C0-BKT-900

HIDING IN THE WORLD

Judith Serin

EIDOLON EDITIONS
SAN FRANCISCO
1998

Copyright © 1998 by Judith Serin

Grateful acknowledgement is made to the following anthologies
and periodicals in which some of these poems have appeared:

New Poets: Women (Les Femmes), Contemporary Women Poets
(Merlin Press), Dear Gentlepersons (Hartmus Press), The
Illuminations Reader, Transfer, Kosmos, Room, Velvet Wings, Bachy,
Illuminations, Gray Sky Review, The Ohio Journal, The Old Red
Kimono, Writer's Forum, Nebraska Review, The Ohio Journal, and
Barnabe Mountain Review.

Library of Congress Catalog Card Number 97-94641

ISBN 0-9661671-0-4

Gratitude is due to my publisher, Diane di Prima, to Betsy Davids,
to Jackie Dennis, to Cathy Colman for twenty-five years of
friendship and help with writing, and to "the group:" Ellery Akers,
Bill Edmondson, Jerry Fleming, and Peter Kunz for twenty-five
years of help as well.

for my family:

In memory of my father, Bernard Serin
to my mother, Bernice Serin
my sister, Joan Serin
and my husband, Herbert Yee

CONTENTS

MY FATHER SPEAKS

WATER AND AIR

HEDGEROWS

THE ANGRY WOMAN IN LOVE

The Lost Dog
for Michael Dennis Browne

1

We are walking in white
Stumbling in white desert
we search for a moving pole
the stars hammered into the sky
Our voices shuttle across the night
Snowdog   Snowdog
You have gone into your name

2

Your voices fall at my feet
and break
I shall not answer you
keepers
blind swimmers on the brink of the world
My name creeps from the snow
I let it be my mother
sniffing in my ear
I let it be frost scratching
on my father's door
You strangers, foolish crows
in my white world
my nest is deep beneath my feet

3

I am a white dog lost in the snow
the stars have come into me to hide

The Angry Woman in Love

A hill here darkens from the top
and bottom
leaving a central line of light
a seam or meeting place

I stand as the sun sets
holding onto myself
air thins
my skin is loosening

I need to touch any man's arms
slide my hand down his stomach
I know there are other bodies
I would be at ease with those bodies

This morning, leaving your house
I fell
skin scraped off my leg in curls
I will not leave flowers on your pillow
no matter how much I want to

Vermeer's Woman with a Water Pitcher
for Mildred Siegel

Glued to this light
I am a part
though I held this arm
differently once
folding linen
stirring sauce
You won't ask
was I married or single
surly or kind

The map is my husband
the pitcher my child

And I, a face
serene and blurred
a larger pearl
outside the chest
won't answer

Still
I don't know why
When I opened the window
that let the lighting in
I was only repeating
one of many gestures
Now, ignorant
I am an angel
more surely than if I had wings

Migrating Birds

1. New Jersey

The birds are noisy leaves
that will not stay
I run to the window
to see the talking tree
The birds fall up
into cloud white sky
already cold as snow

2. Vermont

Vermonters build white houses
because they know
they cannot compete with this color
I walk with my first, disastrous lover
nobody on the roads
I do not notice I wear yellow and black
like the leaves
like the trunks glistening with rain
Running down from the cemetery
I slip in a pile of leaves
and skin my knee

Can I tell you how soft this harsh world is?
How each tree and hill
is set in its place
to welcome you

Love's end as predictable as winter
as surprising as the first snow
Always sorrow
always consolation
always the birds come back

3. California

A wind blows today
opens the sky
hawks climb the currents
waiting to kill

I fill with fear in these sudden hills
where the climate is permanent
where love may last
where death is final
and can come at any time

I'm angry at the rub between people...

I'm angry at the rub between people
distortions through glass
the thin light here is so much more than shadow
fog on hills, a wall
blue over the bay, a window

So many grays here
boards, road, telephone poles, fog thinning into clouds
quiet being alone
but words hum along the wires
houses hold people
demands, refusals,
silence like a shield

Our walls
are etched by voices
Can you hear me?
Do you remember?
so unlike the sky
the path sparrows sketch and erase
at the same time

The trees hold gray, the sky holds gray, the water
the light

Against gray a bush of bristling red flowers
lush as berries

Invitation

Live through a winter with me
turn your thoughts inside the house
until it is a body
and fire in the chimney a heart

At night we touch
our eyes slowly close
snow piles against the windows
slides off the roof like sleep

In the morning
wrapped in white
outside is a universe
we send spaceships into
ourselves, bundled beyond recognizable movement
pushing through the snow with messages

Trees write their lives
in the calligraphy of bones
Each branch on the evergreens bends
pointing us home
We discover stone
the warmth at its center

And spring we don't remember comes
like the moon   fat   far   white

To Cathy Leaving a Man

See the flower
bright on the gray branch
its fat hand   open
exposing a sunburst of sexual parts

Remember how a flower later
shrivels
loses its petals
and you forget it

Something stays
that is green like the leaves
that looks lost
that swells

Some seeds grow green wings
whir in the wind

Some are spears
stuck in fur
to journey on the bear
the cat caught between sleep and the thin
light in its eyes
the fox, uncatchable

Why do I talk about seeds?
Because we can ignore them

We spend so much time looking at other people
his eyes   his hair
All you can see are your strong hands
drowning in your lap

He does not rescue them

Put one on the other
slide up the arm
shoulder
round the neck
luxury of hair

Beneath there is something hard
the back of your neck were your dreams are stored
the front of your head where may enter and leave
what you choose

Dark eyes
from the front your face blooms
from the side it smiles
like the new, slender moon

Orange Tree   Dream

This man who seems to be my husband
has hundreds of orange trees
All day we wade through their smell
our hands sticky with it
We hand each other words like spoonfuls of syrup
Oranges fall on the roof
Night fills up with their growing
turning
the sudden decision to sever
Oranges roll down the stairs
sit on our doorstep
And what we have between us
is round and bright and could be opened into sections
Once I fell asleep on the porch
he covered me with orange blossoms

For Sue

On the first warm day
we walk
you notice scraps on the street
a frayed slip of screen
delicately rusting
glass broken in a heap, small cubes
you cradle in a glossy leaf

Why do you look down today
when birds perch in the neighbor's fig tree
my languid lizard moves in her cage
scrabbling through pebbles?

Today
a supremacy of sun day
I forget dying
and even wanting love
I admire the homes of the rich
plastered with foliage
But you discover tatters
on the cool gray street
You preserve them
say you will make a collage

And I think how fair you are
giving each thing its due
all the little breakables
bringing them into sun

Screen, glass, leaf, eucalyptus button
this strange, inanimate blooming

THE FINDING POEMS

*in memory of Sue Stern
and for Herbert Yee*

1.

Falling in love is scary, and I don't say it, menace, the wind hissing on the horizon, the sounds of the sea far away rocking us to comfort, winter pulling in to dark early days, the unsafe holidays, hysterical joy, cars charging out of the night on some impenetrable family mission.

The family, outside the family, divided we fall, into beds, into strange hard kisses, into that fondness for the impossible, and then the possible love, so alien we must push it away, chasing us into beds of old spectacular lovers who entertain us but will not kiss.

2.

With you I kiss, more than ever before, I who did not kiss married for seven years. I will not say I love you but sometimes I do, looking at your hill across the bay, its ugly, alien tower. I kiss your mouth over and over, soft, a flower. I admire your soul and it is large enough for safety, encompassing the hurtling cars, the sudden, leaping disaster, the rock thrown carelessly. With you I open, I open to love, I will not say I love you, I am brimming with water, fading light, returning, I will not say I love you, I will come back to you.

3.

Rocking in some unnamed comfort, menace or water, water you drowned in, Sue, swam out. You reappear. Nothing is lost but me, looking for you. You reappear in a man. So I love him or do not. I do not know if love is menace or comfort. I want you back, behind your back I talk about you, about him, about love, it must be impossible.

Roads, lead us down roads, I see the country, the impossible trees, there must be a better word for trees: dark trees, dusty trees, hungry trees, trees angling in the water for their shadows.

Back to the city. The man in the city. Is it dangerous that you are similar: one dead, who left me in death; one a man, men leave me too? Man in the city, city of light, of air sending messages because it is so clear, limpid messages from one hill to another, one light to another, the air crisscrossed with lines of light, of messages, windows lit in the dark. The lost garden of Eden, you said, Sue, and how can I say the windows? Say comfort, say rocking, rocking me to comfort, the window, a high cradle, no, a high light. An open door to your parents when you are not sleeping they are out there in the liquid world of lamplight after bedtime. They are near, they have left you some light to call out to, they will come, they will bring the arms, lap sleepy light under the lamp shiny buttons of shells, finger touch touch, finger later elsewhere secret delight, warm like the light, so many things in the warm soup of night floating, it was not frightening then, anchored by light.

4.

Blue blue the sky, grey blue the sky, the hills deepening blue, the concrete fence of the school that keeps them in. So I run away from happiness. The whole world is deepening blue, the hour of walking with you, Sue, the hour of your vanishing, fading into blue. The trees, concrete buildings, fence engulfed in the process of becoming night, going back to you.

Someday I will be there, the unimaginable, the it-can't-be-as-

beautiful-as-the-world, the lost garden of Eden. Sue, we join you, in time
we all join you, our bodies do it for us. And will it be beautiful, where
you are? Will I be happy?

5.

I found a cat today, a parking space, but can I find the words
for you today, for body, tree? My cat lies curled on my bed, so asleep,
white paws, I can love him, though he may walk away from me. Can
I love you? I am angry, you may walk away from me.

Now I have embarked on a voyage to find, to find me in you,
in Sue, in the watery clouds which float above my house. It is bright
on the water today, I am alone on my little boat, no you, or maybe a
tiny you I can hold in my hand and look. But this is not exactly you.
It is the perfect you, so smooth, an amulet. It does not speak. I speak
for it, I tell it hundreds of stories, I tell it its life, I make it adventures,
my hand its little boat, I sway it out into the world, I pull it back up
to my mouth, I will swallow it, swallow perfection. I have eaten it, it
is mine, I do not need you anymore.

Then you come entire into my boat which sways and may
sink. You are standing, water around your feet. You are taller than
me, you bring storms, you bring harbors, ropes, cargo piled on the
dock, people, hundreds of people with their noise, you bring the
world with all its hiding places, all the possible faces of menace and
love.

I will not talk about love. Only that it is possible. I am
tender and angry, why should I love you, who are not perfect? I
must find what is wrong, I love only the body, it will change,
tenderness is not inexhaustible, melting away to bickering, boredom,
criticism, trap. I do not know if this is true. Soon, any day now, the
tears will come, a thousand tears each in its own boat, each an ocean
with its own boat voyaging upon it.

6.

*I try a little bit, try to find you, me, to see how the lamp lights
while the sky still holds light, and the two contradict one another and do
not, for the sky is darker, the reflection of my lamp floats in the sky in my
window, and all these lights keep on speaking to each other, the dialogue
shifting, the darkness shifting, and the green light glows in the courtyard
of the school, and Sue comes on her walk with me when we found the
green light in the courtyard of another school, and all these times keep on
speaking to each other. You are in the courtyard now, Sue, I see you. I
place your body there where it is not in the empty courtyard. Will you sit
on that bench? Will you hunch your shoulders? Will you wear orange
and wine and vanish so thin into your coat? Will you wait for me? Will
you smoke a cigarette? I see you, I have only to decide and I will see you.
I will run out, I will wave my arms and call you, I will carry my cat for
you to pet, we will walk, we will go to the swings and swing. Yes, you are
here, I see you where you are not, I could in a minute, a choice, why
don't I run out? What is that edge between our worlds? I can make you
be here, but stay, do not run out to join you in the past which is right
here, in the future which is right here, in heaven which is right here. My
cat watching in the window, he is furry and fat, almond green eyes that
used to be yellow, his tail, his black ears, he closes his eyes, you were his
friend, you who sit there in the courtyard on the bench in the green light
and are not.*

7.

We float, all I can say is we float through the limpid, lightning-
less sky of the city which is not a city because it also has trees, hills,
cottages, and cabins. The sky becomes our bed where we float always
in blue, always in night—day is difficult—always in the erratic glow of
windows, street lights, stars. We float, we hold hands, and it is easy
to float away with you, float into night, float in and out of sex and sleep,
only day is difficult because nothing will be as easy again as twenty-

three when I believed against all evidence, believed for seven years in love. And daylight means decisions, means words, means life is more than tenderness or passion.

Still in the light, walking not floating, I reach for your hand, good man. Your soul is so tall I might swim in it forever, if I have the courage to leave the ground in broad daylight and leap.

8.

Sue, my good Sue, my loved Sue, my gone Sue, now it is indeed the anniversary of your death, now that the day is blue and the school children are exceptionally noisy and you are not. But that sounds more cynical than I mean, can I be a little angry? Sue, you are and are and are and are not here, where the sky gathers mist in its corners, a few children still slowly leave the school, one carrying a briefcase too seriously for her age, here where I am with a man who reminds me of you, here in the world, yes, I love it, yes, it is its beauty as well as your absence that makes me want to cry today. Sue, the world is happiness, I know though I am sad, under a thin layer, some indistinguishable disguise, some other which I may or may not be able to traverse, the world is happiness and I hope you know, I hope you are there, in the happiness, the part I cannot hold, but maybe touch, see sometimes, the part that you were entirely cut off from, you thought, when you left. Sue, I want you, I who never believed, I who hated all religion, I who flinched from the spiritual, the abstract, I want you in heaven.

If you will not be here, and evidently you will not, though you are sometimes in a tree, the sky, the school yard, so maybe you have taught me possibility that there is other than this ground I stand on, other than the ever beautiful, ever interesting, ever ego-trapped pain. And I shall try to say the unsayable, and if I cannot say it, see it, and if I cannot see it, then, hardest of all, on faith only, believe in it, and I will, Sue, at least will try, if only to believe in you. Because I love you and you cannot be gone. I do not say this in self indulgence, I do not say this in

18

self deception, I do not say this to make things easier for myself, I say this because I know that though you are gone, though I cannot feel you, though your body was ashes and a bone in my hand, though you will not drive around the corner in your small white car, though you will not bring me milk or pet my cats, though you will not talk to me of all the things we talked, though I may never even see you in a dream, Sue, you are not gone, and, Sue, the world is happiness, and you are there, and so I can be too.

I dream of houses...
for Herbert Yee

I dream of houses
light that filters through the high windows
of rooms like years I've lived in

I do not say
I'm happy
but I am
though the children, adolescents
in those rooms
rustle their complaints

I dream of houses
wake
your back beside me
kiss
in the hollow between the wings
my body happy with you
like a dumb sister who is always right

Getting Attached to Objects
for Herbert Yee

You tell me your car was scared
when it was stolen
I remember
the pictures we took
in the wrecking yard
the shell stripped and reassembled
with dented pieces

I try to eat a prickly pear
You announce to the cacti
that I'm eating a baby

You report my old coat
jealous at my neglect
has shoved my new coat off the hanger

When the rice cooker falls
you tell me it's trying to commit suicide
and has been saved by the garbage can
who loves it
You mime its open arms
its look of eager devotion
Yes, I understand
its adoration

You accuse me
of slighting the salt shaker
cry
in the voice of the kettle
You knock on the shells of snails
ask if anyone's home
before you crush them
I decide to sacrifice my basil

We argue about my car
You say it has too many miles
you can't understand why I get attached
to inanimate objects

My car's not inanimate, I answer
She moves

The sheep on these hills...

The sheep on these hills
are not always the same sheep
though indistinguishable
like snow

I cannot fight the invisible
the snake who, tensing his muscles in the grass
looks exactly like the grass
or that day when one cell
may quietly start dividing

There is an immense isolation in pain
no matter how many have gone there
you must go by yourself

Why can't I simply love the world
stay here
shrinking in the sun
animals breathing around me?

NOT UNDERSTOOD: POEMS FROM CHILDHOOD

early ambiguous light
morning sweets   wake up

sugar bowl
all good things come from

forbidden
feet on table
sugar
good   bad
goobad
        Dad
            dy

my sister eats dirt
will die
if I
don't tell

DON'T TELL   DON'T TELL
DON'T TELL   Mom
                    my

tattletale
tail
follow the cat
crawl   become small
climb the trellis
where the rose won't grow

nap
world whirs
sun creeps through the shade
stationed at the window

light holds my head
squeezing specks
blue   red
bled
into brain

or blanket
over my face
stiff   brown
will drown
me in wool

legs twitch
tangle the wool
time sits by my bed
a lump

outside
noises   teasing

birds don't sleep
nor cat
nor vines
swelling in the heavy sun

yellow L of light in bedroom
my parents' word against things in corners
figures dancing
    crawling
belong to dark

fairies in flower skirts
enormous record rolling around my bed
weasel
snakes and men with two noses
many fish

STAY
trick the night

goodnight
sleep tight
pleasant   dreams

my father sings
goodnight ladies

safety slipping
    down the hall

sun full noon
afternoon
no nap
no blanket over my eyes

out in the hot sleeping world
ahh
the swing makes wind

I slip off
want Mommy   an apricot
she appears behind door closed to the heat
dark following her like a cat

WAIT
carry the little orange ear
to the swing

WAIT
push sand   push feet
up in the molten air

WAIT
close eyes
sun's hand
wind's arm
summer's honeysuckle smell

NOW
the taste   a flood
I am in the perfect orange time

I go with my father
to see the new house
a hole

foundation
found   a stone
found   a stick
pound

men make noise
below
the edge of earth

I look down
into my house

it will stand
over a hole
bird on a nest
hatching years

in a red dress
my mother calls me
her hair black and shiny
a cardinal in summer sun

I'm hiding
in the folds of the world
admiring her
she stands on the porch
full in the light of secrets

I feel between the pleats on her skirt
surprised when she stops me

blimp hovering
over mound   in the earth
grass grown
door
to the under

blimp
the over
lighter than air
fat sexy secret
not understood

near
not touching
blimp   knows

I
        break apart
like clouds
        leaving

skunkflower smell
in the woods
pungent, pervasive

a root
signals
yellow and red

warning
another inch invading my bones

I'm giddy
in the higher air

journey to the far place
Indian marks on bark in grove

stream to cross
stepping stones
water slides cold

pull up bank

here there is field
grass is tall
wind tells it things

I am a cat
creeping
up on the few junipers

which watch
make statements
choose to group
      for a reason

light deceives
space deceives
a pheasant flies through our window
dies
a jagged hole

my parents cook the bird

I draw pheasant pictures
look
I paste the feathers
on

neighbor's magnolia tree
stingily gives
a few flowers
a year

they are boats
        floating luminously
on dusk

I swing in the hammock
among mosquitoes
just out of sight of the window

the flowers are fragile
color of ladies' china
        cups
night will drink from them
        stars

like the glassed treasures
in the museum
I can't have them

but may   once
pick one

wondering where to hide it

in the field
     spherical
apple tree
branches curve to ground

we throw apples
up   down

up has better aim
     harder apples
down has rotten apples
     can run away

I go alone
in the soft
before dark

on ground
hidden

in tree   cool house
     curving seats

higher

here   I touch sky
sister   to birds   to stars beginning

savory night soup
of July

    tonight
I do not float in bed
sheets kicked off

we gather after dark

the noisy things
I stay away from
    explode

I take my furry sparkler
a bud
before opening
    danger
rising through its stem

breath ballooning
I touch it to fire
flower noisily
    no pain

white
I pull stars to lawn
    trailing colors

run   wave
write my name on night

in heat
things shift
    shimmering

I walk on the road
stones' fists
pound my feet

ahead a puddle gleams
    goes into air

cornflowers waver
    mirror sky
goldenrod
poisonous to my mother
    the color catching her throat

I go lie
in the corner
by the house
in shade cool grass

in sky
    voyages
of clouds

bottoms of boats islands
    dog
spreading into a line
alligator eating
until its jaws curl back

nothing stays
    but heat
pulling down the day

I see my nose
for the first time
    pink snail
floating in front

nagging
    an itch

between
my house and a neighbor's
    I stand still

I was
    large world
    tree   sky   road

    invisible
folded into the air
like eggs in a cake

    safe
as the nest in the tree
the bird melting on the branch
    submerged in sun

now this boundary
    nose
divides me
from the world
    small fleshy form

night in the clubhouse
many parts
of sleep and waking

long night
	broken
by moon light
like days

ghost stories
candles
the big kids' lascivious shudders
I ignore

resisting
then giving in
to sleep
warm dark
fur   against our skin

later
	gray light
without a source
behind trees
in the not glassed windows

twigs and leaves form faces
they are pirates   I am certain
show the others
	who sometimes believe me
	in these matters

I won't sleep again
while leaves watch

but do
dragged awake by certain hand of sun
    that hides pirates
in the drawers of day
shut seamlessly
    in blue

in school
someone brings shells
from Florida

one   a little boat
is white
has sailed on the path
the moon makes

it curls to teeth
a sea mouth
eating waves

I hold it
polished in my palm
all the words I'll ever learn to read
inside its locked mouth

recess
I linger in

I snail toward the teacher's desk
stand

the shell is in my hand
in my pocket
I'm running
the walls suck in
tongue the hall

        outside
there's too much time to play

in class
the windows vibrate

I'm in a dry place
        looking down

the tops of heads
are question marks

the ocean is a mind
that won't be still
	sends things up
as night sends dreams

I find sparkles
winking on sand

shells
once lived in
dry now
	dreams in day

wind at the ocean
tells us   go away
blows our ice cream
out of its cones

light at the ocean
high clouds   curling
gray
at the edge between
waking and sleep
knowing and not knowing

go deeper
crab trap
with my father
from the dock

pull dream from its night
thought from the warm brown
	back of the mind
a thing with claws
unaccustomed to light

the ocean betrays me
I play with its rolling
am rolled
over   over
    sand   salt
scraped back to beach

I pull soft sand
clawing up to light

MY FATHER SPEAKS

My Father's Death

I can't understand words anymore
only objects
the closed doors on the street that live
wholly on the surface

Will the world ever wet me again?

I swam with my father in Bearcamp Pond
brown, private, warm
Papa Bear making oatmeal on a Coleman
wears an incongruous hat
Where in the world are you?

Somewhere there is a man—
I know there must be—
with a high forehead and curls
a smile
In all the photographs you are smiling

"Measure a man by his heart"
your high school yearbook says
Your heart attacked you?
No, it was tired, more tired than you knew

On some corner, some strange street
you are smiling
In Calcutta, emerging from a tea shop?

The wind has been blowing for two months
on Mt. Israel
blowing your ashes gray as the red you couldn't see

I walk with the camera you bought me
The California green is taking over
strangling the stucco
but in queer collusion with windows, doors

Only my eyes are alive
They conspire with objects on the California streets
They say here the world is right
arranging the scene into signals, signposts
He went that away
away, away

If only I could find you, your image
happily doing
one glimpse
I wouldn't even ask for a letter

Love for the Dead

What can I do with love for the dead?
How can I spend this wealth?
Give it to the deserving living
cheating you
who will say, "No, that's mine?"

I had money in the mattress
when my house caught fire
this love whose object is gone
a letter flying in all the airplanes
never to find a mailbox

I see this love, these riches, wasted
I keep throwing it into holes
It is heavy
and will not leave
I am a hunchback, staggering under my love

What can I do with love for the dead?
Put it in a bank
where it accumulates interest
and four times a year a statement comes
saying, "See, I have increased?"

I didn't know I was carrying anything
Oh, a few coins I spent casually
Love was mixed with anger, indifference, distance
perfectly seasoned—our daily bread
Visits scheduled in the years ahead
Christmas, next summer

And I see you in my mind's eye
and in a dream in my mother's bedroom
you come in a black suit
and I run to hug you

The Tree Is Full of Birds, Trying to Get out

Somewhere in my mind I'm building a kitchen for you
a tree house study with a blanket, a few books
The dead are hermits and ascetics
But will you be there?

In dreams you are jogging toward my window
in a runner's shorts and shirt
You have not gone on a journey
You have gone everywhere

Missing person
not in the bureau or in the dictionary
not in any comic strip, taking off for Siam
The stones in cemeteries are steps to the next generation
You're not there

You're in the tree, trying to get out
you're the bleat escaping from the sheep's stupid mouth

We will never be a family again...

We will never be a family again
A chair with three legs will stand
but not if it started with four

Tall ladder-back New Hampshire chair

I remember:
You fished in the fast stream
that sparkled like hundreds of animals' eyes
every morning—trout
I learned to clean them

When I fished with you—
not trout, just sunnies and bass
from the big rock on the lake—
the first one I caught was small
and I threw it, shaking, back
It fell in the rock's crack, irretrievable

Another time
we two were up early Sunday
to make pancakes

You mixed them
I made them in my special turtle shape
You sang and danced then
lumbering in your pajamas
"Good time Charley"

Such curly hair
a face so solid in my mind
a voice
and all I have to tell you
ask you
all you taught me
and should teach me now

Mountains, sky
remember
hold him

Progress of a Sunset

Edge of day, light in the sky makes the dark world flat, houses on houses. Layers of color float toward me. Birds, clumps of winged earth, fall through them.

Cold outside. Warm behind windows where the lamp makes a yellow sky on my wall and desk. House plants look out through glass, send roots into the air, knowing that earth must be near.

This sky leaves so slowly, like warmth leaving a body. There is time to look for you, who are gone. The dead are hiding in this sky, waiting to be deciphered, like the spider on my hand, lost in the valleys and mountains of warmth.

Doorway to the west glows before it closes. Night is deep, a well we cannot see into, anymore than day's flat face. While it gathers, I am close to you. This is different than dreams. This is here, sharing the world. To look at you, somewhere in these clouds, is almost enough.

Anniversary of Your Death

I'm hiding on the roof from today; it's watching me
from the long apartment house down the block
Today should be any day
a summer day that's so present
it beats you back into the house
It wants to be left alone
to be summer, any summer, any tree heavy with leaves and fruit
        still green

Sitting here, I travel along the telephone wires
slide into the sea
Last night I had a dream in a green amphitheater, June, a
        graduation
an old town, settled
the houses like statues under their big trees
I was angry at a beautiful young man, because he did not come
        closer
I kissed him in front of his mother, to embarrass him

No one can be as close to me as my cat is now
sitting in the shade of my bent knees
No one fits into my life that well
lets me shelter him

What is here:
waterfalls of leaves, pools of shadow
tiles sunning on the roof
a towel flapping in the wind like goodbye
windows with curtains
roofs with windows, the secret lives of attics
inside them—the square of sky
bright ship upon the shadow

I wanted to keep this day open for you
a tunnel for you to come through
But the sky fits too closely to the trees
Buildings poke the air but do not puncture it
Cry
for all this that will probably continue
but, like the bird who perched on a twig and sang two notes
is gone when I look up again

My Father Speaks

Being dead is not so bad
You get used to the faded light
like old photographs
or ink

The world's less brilliant
no day or night
I see you sleeping
I see the fox lift his ears
lope through the listening fields
but the moon's a pat of butter
in the milky sky
Earth does not tug me to sleep

Touch I used to miss
it too has faded
Sometimes a fuchsia flower
pricks me with what is almost pain

Once I saw a tomcat
his pale orange fur matted
rub his scarred head again and again
against a bush
I ached to scratch his chin

This was outside your window
But I don't watch you
Sometimes you call and I try to listen
It's like reading an old letter

I trust you to live
as you are beginning to let me die
I know I walk miniature in your mind
My sayings you have inherited
slip from your tongue

I care less, I suppose
Don't misunderstand
There is still love
but its rays strike oblique
through a dusty pane

WATER AND AIR

A sock left by the road...

A sock left by the road
fills with sunlight
a shed skin that begins its own life

Our leavings
have the dignity of snails
moving slowly into their surroundings

There is a blue scarf
I picked up once in the rain

It took weeks to dry
now languishes in a drawer
too small for any neck

Sun Again

Sun again, after a long rain
A spider running faster than my eye
so small he becomes invisible

Outside my plum tree has done it again
the opposite of vanishing
White blossoms break from black branches, cracks on clouds

I won't see that spider again
so beautifully fast and small

Spider, Invisible's signature
in the corner of my eye
Spider, my father
teasing me from corners

See how the blue sky sank, pushing down the clouds
the top of my tree almost reaching it now
An airplane is fast and small and vanishes

All these little absolutes

I miss the past possibilities most
A day I put on perfume and thought of sleeping with someone new

I have this dream of opening a drawer and discovering photographs
of a new past. Snapshots. I'm smiling. I've grown up with
everyone I now love.

Letter to Calvin

Hello, my friend:

The mountains across the water are soft as haze
water mirrors clouds
from a chimney somewhere smoke lowers the sky

Everything is tremulous
Matter: liquid in a thin skin
We are intruders here
too solid and loud

My cat lies on his side in the sun
a frayed red collar, half closed blue eyes
He is ease
In the morning he sniffs the wind
as if deciding to drink

I'm swimming, I will go back to when you were here, to our
        childhoods when we should have known one another, back
        to my father's childhood; I'll know why he was like you,
        who hadn't been born yet in another country

You are an avocado on the table
landscape on the outside
inside a bath of green
the large yellow heart
that will grow

Windy Spring Day

1.

Windy spring day
my plum tree has turned green
no longer surprises me with that white out the window
a near cloud

The clouds are not near now
but present
gray on gray
a school of porpoises drifting
in light so low
we all are under water

And in me my loves
are swimming up to feed
their mouths tickling
the underside of thought
their eyes shiny and opaque

My room is more than ever a ship
in this stormy weather
Trees outside click in the wind
like kisses
They have reason to love me

2.

Raindrops now
letters
to my lettuce
My lettuce is growing
in its box
under the soil
growing too
secretly and more elaborately than its leaves

Under the soil
I am growing
who knows what roots
and all my loves are rain
falling
through the soft gray sky

Fly

On the brink of being able to

my bones turning whiter
the moon a licked bone in the sky

This spring night came without a winter
while I waited for snow
the plum trees flowered white

The Japanese photographer of the Himalayas
does not believe in mountains
unless they are covered with snow

He photographed a desert to look like ice
the Himalayas like clouds

To me they are heaven, in which I do not believe

We are comforted in spite of ourselves
in spite of ourselves we will fly

HOMES OF THE STARS

*This series is based on a set of postcards
from the seventies with photographs of the
actors' houses and small insets of the
actor's faces.*

Home of Jimmy Durante

It looks like a motel
crowned with a palm tree like Carmen Miranda's hat
Jimmy wants to sell us something
The car in the driveway?
A station wagon, practical for the family
He's scared
his eyes glancing up to watch the back of his head
He tries so hard to please us

Home of Lucille Ball

Orderly
everything goes in threes
trees like columns, hedges, window boxes on dormer windows
even the house number:
three zeros after an incidental 1

Her head is straight on her slanted shoulders
eyes alert but calm
fruit-like lips closed

A cross rises from her roof, disturbing the peace
a straggly T.V. antenna
fragile, undignified, askew

Home of Debbie Reynolds

Where she lives is sexual and closed
door like an angular vulva
two posts and a dark opening
no windows, but a long expanse
of geometric texture
that irritates/arouses
eye and fingertip

Palm trees sprout from one center on cylindrical stalks
In the foreground, the heart-shaped leaves
wiggle their fingers
Flat sky a hand on the back of the neck
shadow deep and moist

Home of Paul Newman
and Joanne Woodward

A fortress for coupledom
will they be safe
behind the white brick fence
the tree with many trunks
joined like an elephant's foot
firmly on the lawn?

The front seems a facade
set at a slant to draw our eyes away
from the curtained bay windows
the massive creamy solidness
of the place

Foliage creeps up
secretive ivy, showing brown roots
A fern tree fans its wings
In the shadows the lilies
multiply
their smooth leaves spear-like
At the roof an oval curves
tall enough for a person to stand in

Joanne and Paul stand together
his head is slightly larger
turned toward profile
their eyes have the same sincerity
hers darker, more guarded
their lips set
in firm closed smiles

Home of Doris Day

It might be haunted
a big house with trapezoidal roofs
the urns, overpowered, like ashtrays on the fence
the one open window
an escape route
treasure or body buried under the tree

The star, meanwhile
looks at us sideways, eyebrows lifted
squeezed smile
safe
to entice
hands folded under her chin

Home of Dean Martin

He has manufactured New England
even imported the clouds
The trees wave for help
in the shallow soil
have obligingly lost their leaves
They march in a row, four soldiers

We know the wind blows
a crisp day
the barn must be behind
a setter lopes figure eights in the field

The star's face is half in shadow
a cloud or airplane flying over
he squints into the distant sun

Home of Barbara Stanwyck

Her head is about to topple
glued
where the shadow or ribbon bands her neck
Is she victim of some monstrous operation?
Eyes turn up as head tilts down
Her mind, disconnected
revolves under the swirled hair

See how ominous the curve of the drive
A lamp shaped like a shrine
too short to light the way for anyone but dogs
wears a black hat
a black number—718—bordered in black
a funeral announcement
Shadows stain the lawn

The house is inconspicuous
a low roof broods
over the many-paned windows
There by the door is something red
glistening, bleeding

Home of George Burns

An ante-bellum mansion
the savannah tree
spreads in front, sectioning the sky
lacy ironwork on the balcony
where Scarlett steps

From its imposing front
the house glides back to servants' quarters
small rooms perfectly square
one window in each
a perfect square of blue
a place for mathematical serenity
Triangular white bricks march beside the drive
bones of years

George is quietly proud
class president in the high school yearbook
serious, but not unfriendly
eyes curved slits of fellowship

Home of Burt Lancaster

In the Spanish style
tiles, a spiky plant, fortress door
the lawn a pale patch invaded by trees
A path runs to the porch, pauses
There will be/has been a war here
a messenger, red-caped
pounds the door with the hilt of his sword
then dies or kills the lord

Burt will not tell us the story
his jaw so square his mouth cannot possibly open
He stares over our heads
far to the future or past

Home of Fred MacMurray
and June Haver

Colonial
half buried behind trees, heaps of ivy
A chimney undulates up one wall
We imagine the large open room, beamed ceiling
chairs clustered around the warmth of the fireplace
after our day of raking leaves
and strolling through the cemetery

Even the picket fence
seems authentic
Snow will cap the posts in perfect cones
for mittened fingers to slide through
Quiet clings to the house

Fred's tie is boisterously L.A.
like his shark's smile
June also smiles, but her lips are closed
She's so much smaller
the pearl at her ear a pool of memory

Home of Groucho Marx

His front yard is a desert
with an oasis of palm trees near the wall
red flowers a carpet at their feet

The hedge is a caterpillar
the bush a sentinel
or his hat
Japan in the scattered stones
the bonsai maple
draped in autumnal orange

A bougainvillea humps the roof
a green hill hovers above
The house is long, low, white
the openings covered with circular grillwork
a trap for the eyes
guarding the Sultan's harem
the pretense of the ordinary
that keeps us out

Inside it's dark and cool
secrets in the star's shiny head
the smile of a snake about to strike

Home of Jimmy Cagney

English, half-timbered
many peaks and a T.V. antenna
pierce the sky
A spiny bush leans against the house
a shaggy rhododendron looms
like a drunken guest
The hedges have cowlicks
a large urn on the doorstep
is sure to collect trash

The colors—white and rust
connote breeding
but the lawn for all its manicure
is olive drab
the shadow of a leafless tree
reaches for the house

We do not believe the butler
will serve tea
and enormous, awful breakfasts
Jimmy is too small
his hat too slanted
He looks so trustingly up
a bird chirping to morning

Home of Jack Benny

There are dark places
on this house set firmly in the sun
A net of shadows
fishes the emerald lawn
the Georgian windows like pools
unrippled, unreflecting surfaces
We are reluctant
to step into the empty, open-mouthed garage
a tunnel
too long to show the light

Shadows of eaves and chimneys slant
carving corners
The house is a puzzle we cannot solve
a few curves and flourishes
thrown haphazardly at its facade

Jack's smile tyrannizes his face
his right shoulder humped
almost to his eyes
which, embarrassed, glide from our gaze
Water would slip off him easily
he is so round and smooth

Hospital Poem

It's nice in the hospital
people bring you things
flowers   which wink   opening one by one
to the nurses' admiration
tubular, pink   like viscera

You abdicate
to sheets so white they shriek
They are arctic   those sheets   so clean
no crumbs or love stains or cat hair
no ink marks from writing dreams in bed
no dreams   but the Demerol day
where the mind stumbles between future and past
or stalls forever on the sunny window sill
sun on glass   sun on glass   sun...
Is that how life shuts off   simple as T.V.?

Food comes   of little interest
your appetite   for the shots
regular as clockwork   a chime of pain
The needle softened by your need
you cannot feel the bruises
it spreads on your skin
Time ebbs   the flowers cupping light
fade into night

Do the nurses laugh softly in the halls?
No, they earn this gravity
they earn a living
bringing love every three hours on a tray

Drive by the hospital and wave
hello
Demerol   Demerol
rehearsal

Does a Fish Have a Word for Water?

"the never mind grave"
Cathy Colman

1.

Ninety-five Nevermind, mean old man, scowls through my dreams. Never mind you won't find water the eye swims in before you stuff the soil. Slip down the hall into oblivion. See the bare turkey on the other side of the door: large, awful, pink. I want a word to touch all the leaves on top of the tree. Behind my back sky plots its escape, leaving no trees, teeth, no mirror, song. Never mind.

2.

When I look in the mirror dream, I'm not there. My lover peers from the edge. The center silvers nothing. No thing, we have inherited no thing. We don't know what a cat knows about sun. Lost: the art of going without dents.

3.

In a dream I chase a friend through a door. Her hat, clothes at the top of the stairs, but she has another face. Everyone you love changes into someone else, sporting a little souvenir—eyes, voice, smile—like a necklace she forgot to leave you.

4.

Sky multiplies, multiplies. Sometimes I see a number. Sometimes I see, sink into saucers of light. The river has birds. The clouds, fat, have weight in the sky. Seeing is a shiver up the spine. Wind has no sides.
Stretch to be the hose water slips through. Transparent, the mind turns around.

How an Ark Goes on the Water

Water and air
they carry you

The ark, the house upon the water
dinners interrupted by waves
the animals disorderly
At first always rain
containing them, a cradle

Then sailing into the mountains
perilous navigation
Top of the world
where birds float on polar ice
green as though it grew the cold

But they can't stay there, no fields to grow the grain
So they go on, a life upon the water
domestic now
the animals orderly as careful children
each waiting its turn to dip in the rainwater barrel and drink
everyone with a favorite spot in the sun
Each morning they lean head and bare arms over the edge to wash
scoured by salt

They come to desert country
the mountains brown, rising out of the water
But the sun is farther than before the flood
when it shoved travellers against the sand
It weeps lemon tears, blanching the sky

Drifting, they see the jungle mountains, Andes
gray stone that supports a continent like a spine
the cloud mountains, Himalayas
unapproachable purity
They only dare raise their eyes to them
when a sunset showers them with blood

They grow clean on the water
forgetful
They can't tell their children from the animals'
Wind sweeps out their thoughts
They turn solid, pocked and smoothed like stones
The past wears away bit by bit
into immense distances

Immense distances
travelling the world, the world being underwater
What they cannot see:
the temples of Kuala Lumpur, the hanging gardens of Babylon,
    Stonehenge—
man's towers and trenches, monuments to gods and wars

What they see:
The monuments of the earth
where it has pushed a mountain to celebrate some vast pressure
a fist of heat or cold
The clouds' migrations
drifting on shades of blue, an instant evolution
The ocean—a bridal veil, a road, a bed—
the waves, landscape correcting itself
sky and sea like a face and body happy with each other
necklaces of birds
continents of color
gray blanket, blue mirror, green pasture
the sound and smell lodged in their ears and noses
rhythm of thought, flavor of dreams
immense distances

They learn loneliness
love of water
they learn that time comes back upon itself, a snake dappled by
        days
that death is solid as the mountains
and the future floats around them
that sex is water dripping on a pebble
that stones grow and die

They learn of fish
of grace and lovely, edible flesh

Then their ticket runs out
First the bird with the olive branch—
they haven't seen a tree in years—
They turn it in their hands:
low country

Soon they find it
slopes with grass they can step out on
They stay in the ark for days on receding water
stretch their arms farther each morning to touch it

Finally one puts a foot on the earth, which resists
They fall, are bruised by a world that will not hold them
crawl into the hills already unfolding with wheat

They find they are a woman and a man, getting old
The trees hurt their eyes and stop the sky
Every day their children build bigger their cage

Do they drown then in the flood of progeny, farms, towns
that rise around them?
Or do they, as legend states, slip one day
into a river that carries them out to a bay and beyond?

HEDGEROWS

to Peter Beales with gratitude for his books on roses

Winter

An English gardener walks through the fields in winter. His wife is a hungry sparrow, his children crows pecking on the floor of his heart. They fill the world with noise: clicks and squawks; movement: wings beating, hops into the air, flurries of fighting over the larger pieces of grain. Where has his love gone? In what seed or root? The sky is a weight, the earth hunkered down, frost white fingers in the ruts the tractors made. The sun shivers. He can't remember spring budding or summer pouring over the land.

Here is a hedgerow, a thicket of gray branches, lusterless leaves, thorns. Thorns! Blood on his fingertip. Shoots of new green tinged with red. Canes of a rose, twenty feet long, woven through. *Rosa arvensis.* Soon the silver pink cups of the Ayshire rose Splendens will spill the scent of myrrh. Here is a gate at the end of the hedgerow. Will he go through?

Starfish

A woman walks with her husband to a beach. He reads while she explores the tide pools. Gray sky, weak sun, but a world in the moving water. She finds starfish, a reward for going to the beach her husband chose, though he won't come out on the rocks with her. She looks, then walks. It is getting dark. She feels alone. Sometimes her husband seems far away; a good friend died recently; another is entangled in a difficult romance and doesn't call. But the starfish are a gift. What do they mean? In her mind she sees them spin into the darkening sky. Drops of light string between them, to her. But no, she thinks, I don't want such a distant connection; I don't want to look up so far. I want to work in my garden. Then she remembers that the sun is a star. All the people in her life are stars, connected by these beads of light. She looks into the night sky and wonders if she will remember this.

Sky

A girl lies on her back in the snow. She isn't cold. She looks up through branches at the sky. Is heaven there? It is far away. The branches above her are far as well, too high to climb. A bird lands in one, a chickadee. It turns its head to look at her. Flies away. But it has brought the branches closer. They make a pattern like a jigsaw puzzle, become the cracks between the sky, which is here now—she reaches out her arm to touch it, icy blue. She closes her eyes, opens them; the sky recedes. Closes and opens them again; it returns. Heaven is caught on the bare twigs, hiding in the world. She is in it. She closes and opens her eyes.

Spring

     In spring the English gardener cleans the old greenhouse where his father worked, abandoned now, much of its glass broken. He is going to tear it down, put up a modern one. Why has he waited so long, until he absolutely needed the space? Why is he on his hands and knees, shifting through piles of debris? There is nothing here.

     But how can it all be gone? The potted begonias his father loved, their papery petals translucent in the white-washed light. The rose cuttings in gold-flecked vermiculite, sticks from all over the world, labelled in his father's formal, rounded hand. His black notebooks, filled with that handwriting: notes on experiments with culture, the weather, breeding, and even his joy at a Felicity covered with pink roses stirring scent into the air. And where is the hand that wrote those notes? Long fingers, skin cracked, dirt in the lines and under the fingernails no matter how often they were scrubbed. It is all so alive in his mind, the stacks of pots lined on the benches clearer than his father's face.

     His father's face. No, he cannot see it. He cannot hear his father's voice teaching the visitors who came to admire, so unusually loquacious that he always tagged along at the outskirts of the group to hear. Gone. Not even a shard of pottery in the heap of dirt and broken glass. He should watch out for his hands, sweep this mess up with a broom. Toss it into the trash.

     He rises, hands on his back. Something brushes his shoulder. He startles, turns. The cane of a rose growing in through the cracked roof. La Mortola—single, white, the petals coming to a curious point at the end of their curve like a Moorish temple. He was eight when they planted the cutting carried home from the famous garden. It will grow over the greenhouse, his father said. He can hear him saying it.

Animals

The woman is alone at night, her husband working late. It is a balmy evening, warm for early spring, and she is thinking of her friend who died at the start of winter. It hurts her that Sue will not see the light come back this year. She walks into the kitchen. Why is there a dead leaf in her sink? No, it's a newt with a purple-brown back and orange belly. Its head is tilted, its eyes dark bumps. She picks it up and brings it outside, wet pads scuttling on her palm, then stoops to put it in the garden where it blends with the dark. She rises into the light of the porch lamp lining the leaves of a nearby tree and is face to face with an opossum, grasping the trunk, head down, watching her with its round black eyes. Neither moves. She stays for a long time, nods, and steps back into the house. The air is furred with hidden movement, vibrating with a sound just below the level of her hearing; she pushes through it as she goes to sit in her stuffed chair. She remembers: those were her friend's favorite animals. "Sue?" she calls.

Lawns

The girl sits on her porch. The lawns are empty. Why is she so lonely, so ill at ease? Has she been dropped from another planet to this place? She stares at the spot where lawn meets trees. A border. The dark breathing, taking on form. Out of the woods steps a tall creature, its fur polished mahogany catching sunlight. Yeti, she calls. It puts a finger to its lips, then waves. Three others emerge from the trees, cross the lawns. They come together, dance, a graceful lumbering, lifting huge feet, waving arms toward the sky. The first one stops, looks at her, beckons. Will she run across the lawns to them, stumbling on the gravel road? Will she dance?

Summer

The English gardener walks, searching for the eglantine, *R. eglanteria*, its leaves scented of apple. A species rose given by the soil, growing wild over hedgerows, into trees, uncultivated. He is thinking of how his father was so much more distinguished than he, travelling around the world discovering species, breeding new roses, named after himself, his wife, but not his son.

Now the gardener needs some word from him, some reassurance that, at fifty, he has not wasted his life, that not only is he accomplished, but also loved. Strange that he needs to know he is loved: he has a wife; he has five children; he has always assumed that he is. But now he needs love from someone else. From his father? From himself? From the earth, the hard packed clay he steps on, the sinuous trunks of vines growing into the hedgerows, the green that covers everything.

The first rose I come to will be me, he thinks, will be my father's message, what he thinks of me. Some delicate wild rose, he hopes, or some old garden rose heavy with petals and scent, still blooming where a cottage stood a century ago. The path turns a corner. High over a hedge something red, bright, insistent. Yes, it is a rose: Altissimo. Modern, huge single petals, no fragrance. A ferocious rose, tough and thorny, pushing to the sun, growing in wind, in dry soil, without water, from a few sticks thrust in the ground. A survivor, strong and blunt as summer.

Trails

The woman has come back on vacation to Wonalancet Intervale. It is where she goes in her mind when she needs calm: a grassy field; a white church with a steeple at the edge of a stand of trees; a ridge curving over three hills—Wonalancet, Hibbard, Hedgehog—the names here are an incantation; and the four peaks behind, the distinctive profile of a mountain range. She has climbed them all.

Then she sees something else: the dirt track where the road curves past the church. She follows it through the woods to an opening. How could she have forgotten this? Ferncroft, the trail head, where all the hikes up the mountains begin. The scene spreads before her: A farmhouse with a shed to its side placed delicately on the green meadow that starts the rise; the trees where the wooden signs point the ways up the mountains. The ridge. And the mountains: the promise of their height; the dark rocky trails where she watched her feet, finding Indian pipe, beechdrops, mushrooms, trillium, and Solomon's seal; the push through beech and birch to spruce, dark with needles; then the open ledges, sheets of granite, the summits. Top of the world, peaks and hills and farms and lakes spread around her; the air above the treeline cleaner, more delicious than anything else.

Whiteface, Passaconaway, Paugus, Chocorua. She remembers when she learned she wanted to climb them. She hiked with her family to Blueberry ledges. They often collected fruit there, but this time they went farther up the trail to a view of the summit—the cliffs, the white face, huge, close. A presence. I want to go there, she thought, learning something about herself.

Now she knows why she had forgotten Ferncroft. Magic must remain hidden. The intervale, so solid in her mind, is the place to rest and gather oneself for the climb. She will always remember it, but Ferncroft will fade, rearrange itself, trick her, keep its secrets, keep hers.

Brambles

The girl walks out alone in summer heat that shimmers off the gravel road in sheets like water. It is noon, indoor weather, but she is bored. She brushes through the cornflowers at the side of the road, thinking they are fallen chips of sky. She steps into the woods where the yetis live, but doesn't expect to see them today in this sleepy heat. There is something that disturbs her. Far back in the trees a patch of earth has been cleared. She came upon it one day in spring. It was stark, a square of reddish brown shale. She walked around it, trying to seal it.

Now she heads toward it, wondering if she will find the skeleton of a new house, those raw boards standing up in emptiness, suggesting structure, so menacing yet tempting to climb, though she has been warned not to. The woods are drooping with heat. Thick vines like snakes wrap the trees. She wants to touch them, but always the sly glisten of poison ivy scares her off.

Then she is there. No boards. But the earth is not bare. Brambles have crept across it—dark rough leaves, thorns, later there will be blackberries, shiny sweet. She steps into the square, kneels, carefully lifts a cane with the tips of her fingers. More underneath, gripping the ground. She feels the roots reaching down, connecting under the surface. The branches, too, connect, grasping each other. They rise into green bodies, spreading over emptiness. Bramble people with shy green eyes. She turns her head and they sink into a disorderly push of leaves and thorns. But they are there, reaching to her.

Fall

At dusk in fall the English gardener walks between hedgerows and wonders why little things hurt him now—a callous dismissal from an adolescent son, his wife's preoccupation when he wants to talk. There is no need, but rage rises. As though he were four again and weren't allowed to sit with the guests after dinner. Old wounds. Are they ever gone? A moth flops toward a tree. What light is it looking for? The moon is rising, huge and flat over a cottage roof, nearly full, but with a chunk bitten out of its side. It climbs the tree, whose branches are almost leafless but hung with fruit: apples, perhaps, or pears. He sees his wound there—thick trunk, then branching to smaller limbs, twigs. It bears fruit. He must not want it gone.

Leaf

The woman visits her childhood home, long belonging to another. She does not knock on the door but walks quietly around the side, past the crab apple tree she sat in all summer when she was twelve, down into the woods, squeezing between trees she used to slip through, to the stream at the bottom of the hill. She bends carefully on the bank, afraid of poison ivy. The water flows, as it has always flowed, as it flowed for thirty years in her absence. Shoals of rounded stones, reddish mud, debris snagged around a black branch.

She sees a leaf; it swirls in an eddy. A brown leaf, oval, pointed at the end. It floats away. Leaf leaves. She remembers a line from *Walden: Time is but the stream I go a-fishing in.* She sang that when she was sixteen, falling in love with the words with the passion that teenagers can displace to anything, to the tune of "Juanita:" *Nita, Juanita, broke my heart that we're apart.* Why does everything float away? She wants to hold time still in her hand, a fist of water.

She puts her fingers in the stream; the current nudges them. Remembers the life she found there—crawfish, tadpoles, minnows she caught in a pot and pretended to cook. Things move; the stream carries them to the river—she thinks of a picture book she read when she was five—the river to the ocean. A white sailboat. A huge white ocean liner streaming away. Why isn't she on it? She's here by the stream, her hand in rippling water. A leaf has floated away. Somewhere, upstream, a leaf drops from a tree. Floats toward her.

Years

The girl walks down her road and finds a pile of leaves. Should she jump in? No, it looks like someone's house. She kneels, hoping to see what's inside as she would an Easter egg with a window at one end. Leaves—texture and color—she closes her eyes to feel their crispness in her hand. She sees inside: flowers sleep in their bulbs—crocus, narcissus. These are my years, she thinks. All the blooming that will happen in my life. And the house waiting too; someday I will sleep and grow flowers from my fingertips.